AUSTRALIAN SHEPHERDS

by Tammy Gagne

Consultant: Sheila Dolan
Managing Editor,
The Australian Shepherd Journal

Capstone press®

Mankato, Minnesota

Edge Books are published by Capstone Press,
151 Good Counsel Drive, P.O. Box 669, Mankato, Minnesota 56002.
www.capstonepress.com

Library of Congress Cataloging-in-Publication Data
Gagne, Tammy.
    Australian shepherds / by Tammy Gagne.
    p. cm. — (Edge books. All about dogs)
    Includes bibliographical references and index.
    Summary: "Describes the history, physical features, temperament, and care
of the Australian shepherd breed" — Provided by publisher.
    ISBN 978-1-4296-3364-2 (library binding)
    1. Australian shepherd dog — Juvenile literature. I. Title. II. Series
SF429.A79G34 2010
636.737 — dc22   2008055114

Editorial Credits
Jennifer Besel and Molly Kolpin, editors; Veronica Bianchini, designer;
    Marcie Spence, media researcher

Photo Credits
AP Images/Billings Gazette, Casey Riffe, 5 (back)
Capstone Press/Karon Dubke, cover, 1, 5 (front), 13, 16, 21, 25, 27, 28, 29
Corbis/Bettmann, 10
Getty Images Inc./Carl Mydans/Time Life Pictures, 9
iStockphoto/DaydreamsGirl, 14; ginastancel, 22; Tatiana Boyle, 19
Nature Picture Library/Petra Wegner, 7
Newscom, 24
Peter Arnold/Diez, O., 23
Shutterstock/Condor 36, 17; Sergey I, 6; Theresa Martinez, 11, 15

Table of Contents

CHAPTER 1

ACTIVE AUSSIES

Give an Australian shepherd a flock of sheep, and it will round up every one in just minutes. Because of their great herding skills, many Australian shepherds can be found on farms and ranches across the United States. But Aussies, as they are often called, do many other types of work. Aussies work as guide dogs for people who are blind or deaf. Others work as therapy dogs, comforting people who are sick. Some Australian shepherds work as drug-sniffing dogs at airports or as search-and-rescue dogs.

Aussies make wonderful pets for the right people. These dogs are very loyal to their human family members. But these lively dogs need active and energetic owners. Australian shepherds need lots of regular exercise.

Aussies have the skill to herd sheep or cattle.

Is an Aussie Right for You?

Because they need so much exercise, Australian shepherds do best in homes with lots of space. A big yard with a fence is ideal. But an owner should not simply leave an Aussie outside all day to entertain itself. This breed needs to interact with its owner. If left alone too much, an Aussie will surely get into trouble.

Owners should play with their dogs as much as possible.

For a high-quality puppy, go to a good breeder.

The best place to find a puppy is through a responsible breeder. Breeders raise Aussies to be healthy and friendly. You may also find a wonderful adult Aussie through a shelter or breed rescue group. Sadly, many Australian shepherds are surrendered to shelters and rescue organizations. Their original owners did not realize how much time and training these dogs need.

CHAPTER 2

AUSTRALIAN SHEPHERD HISTORY

You might assume that the Australian shepherd breed comes from Australia. But it didn't. The Australian shepherd was developed in the United States.

Many people believe the Aussie's ancestors came from a place called the Basque region. The Basque region is an area of the Pyrenees Mountains between Spain and France. Aussies may be related to a breed called the Basque shepherd. The Basque was brought to the United States in the 1800s from Australia. This may explain how the Australian shepherd got its name.

Australian shepherds did not become popular in the United States until the late 1940s. Farmers and ranchers used Aussies as herding dogs. Over time, they further developed the breed into the intelligent dogs we know today. No one knows for sure which dog breeds were used to develop today's Australian shepherd. Some people think that a type of herding dog from Great Britain was crossed with early Aussies. It is also possible that the German Coulie was used.

Australian shepherds work with ranchers to herd animals like cattle.

Famous artist Norman Rockwell enjoyed the company of Aussies.

Along with herding, Aussies have a history of performing with cowboys in rodeos, horse shows, and movies. These dogs make great performers because they are so loyal and trainable.

EDGE FACT

An Australian shepherd named Chance won the Crufts Dog Show in 2006. This dog show is the world's largest. It is held every year in England.

Australian shepherds have now lived and worked in the United States for more than half a century. The Australian Shepherd Club of America (ASCA) formed in 1957. Twenty years later, a **breed standard** was written. The American Kennel Club (AKC) did not officially accept the breed as a member of their herding group until 1991. Since then, the Aussie has become quite popular. By 1997, the breed was number 40 out of 157 on the AKC's list of most registered breeds. In 2007, it rose to number 33.

Many people choose the loyal, lively Aussie for a pet.

breed standard — the physical features of a breed that judges look for in a dog show

CHAPTER 3

BEAUTY AND BRAINS

Not everyone was happy when the AKC first recognized the Australian shepherd. Many breeders and owners worried that competing in **conformation** classes would spoil the Aussie breed. They thought people might focus on the dogs' appearance instead of their abilities as herding dogs.

But having Aussies in shows has not softened the breed. The breed standard was written with the Aussie's herding abilities in mind. Both the Aussie's look and talents have remained the same since the breed's introduction into the AKC.

A Mid-Size Dog

Male Australian shepherds stand from 20 to 23 inches (51 to 58 centimeters) tall. Females are often a bit shorter. Aussies should be slightly longer than they are tall.

Aussies are solidly built. Their muscular bodies are well balanced. Regardless of its gender, an Aussie should never appear too bulky or too delicate.

conformation — how well a dog meets its breed standard

Aussies are medium-sized dogs with muscular bodies.

Physical Features

Aussies come in many colors and patterns. Colors include black, red, blue merle, and red merle. Merle is a pattern made up of dark-colored patches on a lighter background. Some Aussies have copper-colored markings called tan points. Black or red Aussies with white markings and tan points are known as tricolored dogs.

No two Australian shepherds look exactly alike. Even dogs with the same color pattern can appear quite different. Eye color also varies among Aussies. Eyes can be brown, blue, or amber. The eyes can also include flecks of other colors.

Even Aussie puppies have bright eye colors.

EDGE FACT

Some American Indian tribes called Australian shepherds "ghost-eyed dogs" because of the breed's vivid eye colors.

An Australian shepherd's ears are triangular. When an Aussie is listening to something, its ears perk up with a small flap hanging down. In dog shows, judges subtract points for ears that stand straight up or hang down completely.

An Aussie's tail should not be longer than 4 inches (10 centimeters). Some dogs have naturally short, or bobbed, tails. Breeders usually dock tails that are too long. This means they cut away part of the tail within the first few days of a puppy's life. The original purpose of docking was to prevent a dog from injuring its tail while working. Today the practice is continued because of tradition.

An Aussie's ears give the dog a playful look.

Temperament

Australian shepherds are friendly dogs, but they can also be suspicious of strangers. The best way to make an Aussie feel at ease around people is to socialize it. Take your dog to meet as many people as possible while it is young.

Aussies are very intelligent. Training is easy, but dogs cannot train themselves. If left untrained, any dog will likely learn bad behaviors, like chewing on furniture. To prevent this, many owners take their Aussies to **obedience** classes.

Aussies need to be trained in order to have good behavior.

obedience — obeying rules and commands

Aussies are also loyal dogs. They will give their all to protect the people they love. An Aussie needs good training so it can understand the difference between people who are playing and those who are fighting.

Aussies can be aggressive when herding livestock. But they are just doing their job. Most Aussies are very gentle with their human family members. They get along well with children. However, parents must be aware of this breed's strong herding instinct. If left in a room with lively kids, an Aussie might start rounding up the children like sheep!

EDGE FACT

In the past, Australian shepherds have been called Spanish shepherds, pastor dogs, bob-tails, blue heelers, New Mexican shepherds, and California shepherds.

Dog Shows and Events

Many Aussies compete in organized events like obedience, agility, or fly ball. In obedience, dogs show their ability to follow commands through a series of exercises. Agility is a canine sport in which dogs run over or through obstacles. In fly ball, teams of dogs compete against each other in relay races. Each dog jumps on a lever to release a ball into the air. The dog then runs after the ball to catch it before it hits the ground.

Aussies may also participate in herding events. These activities turn the Aussie's oldest job — gathering sheep or other livestock — into fun contests with other herding dogs.

Although this breed is best known for its herding abilities, the Australian shepherd is also beautiful. Aussies that closely match the breed standard compete in dog shows. Judges rank the show dogs by comparing them to the breed standard.

Lively Aussies love running around agility courses.

CHAPTER 4

CARING
FOR AN
AUSTRALIAN SHEPHERD

Owning an Australian shepherd is not for everyone. This high-energy breed needs plenty of exercise and regular grooming. Caring for an Aussie can also be expensive. Athletic breeds may need to eat more food than less active dogs. As with any dog, owners must also pay for regular veterinary care.

Feeding

Two Australian shepherds can eat very different amounts of food each day and still remain healthy. The amount of food you give your Aussie should be based on several factors. Your dog's height, age, and activity level all play a role in how much your dog should eat. A dog that participates in herding or agility contests will require more calories than less active Aussies.

Most Australian shepherds need a food made specifically for active dogs. This type of food can be found at your local pet supply store. Foods made for active pets contain more calories and **protein** than regular foods.

A good diet is important for the health of your Aussie.

protein — a nutrient that keeps muscles strong and the body healthy

Exercise

Australian shepherds need more exercise than most dog breeds. A simple walk around the neighborhood each day is not enough for them. If your Aussie is not involved in a sport, it must get lively playtime each day.

If you have a fenced yard, use it to run around and play with your pet. Most Aussies love to play fetch. Many Aussies also enjoy playing in water. In warm weather, swimming is a great way for your Aussie to get exercise.

Swimming is a fun way to exercise your Aussie.

Learning to track is fun for your dog and provides good exercise.

Competing in tracking and carting events is another way for Aussies to get exercise. Dogs can practice their search-and-rescue abilities during tracking activities. To earn a tracking title, a dog must follow a person's scent over a long distance. Carting is a traditional activity in which dogs haul carts filled with various items like firewood.

Grooming

Owners must make time to groom their Australian shepherds. Luckily, grooming is not difficult. Aussies' coats do not mat easily, and they never need to be trimmed. Since dried mud falls off Aussies, they don't often need baths. Even farm dogs only need to be bathed once every couple of months.

Aussies only need baths once in awhile.

Brush your Aussie's coat weekly. Brushing removes dirt from a dog's coat. It also helps prevent shedding. Aussies shed hair all year long. But owners may notice that their dogs shed even more in spring and fall. During these seasons, most Aussies need daily brushing.

You will also need to trim your Aussie's nails and brush its teeth. Nails should be clipped every few weeks. Teeth should be brushed every day. Chewing marrow bones can help remove plaque and tartar from your dog's teeth. Never use toothpastes made for people on your Aussie. Human products can make dogs sick.

EDGE FACT

Every Aussie owner should have a slicker brush. This tool looks like a wire hairbrush. It is great for removing dead hair.

Veterinary Care

To keep your Australian shepherd healthy, take it to a veterinarian, or vet, at least once a year. At your Aussie's checkup, the vet will weigh your dog, take its temperature, and listen to its heart. Your dog will also receive any necessary **vaccinations**.

Having a vet spay or neuter your Aussie will help it reach an old age. These simple operations prevent dogs from having puppies. Fewer unwanted puppies help control the pet population. Spaying or neutering also reduces the animal's risk for many health problems, including cancer.

Australian shepherds are generally very healthy animals. Like all breeds, though, they are prone to certain problems. Some Aussies suffer from hip dysplasia. The hips of a dog with this condition do not fit together properly. Hip dysplasia causes pain and makes movement difficult.

vaccination — a shot of medicine that protects animals from a disease

Vet visits are an important part of caring for your Aussie.

EDGE FACT

Australian shepherds can live 15 years or more.

Some owners say their Aussies wag their entire lower bodies to make up for their short tails.

A Devoted Dog

Owning a dog is a big responsibility. Owning an Australian shepherd is an even greater one. These smart and lively animals require a lot of time and care. From feeding to exercising, caring for an Australian shepherd will be a big part of each day. But the care and attention you give your dog will be worth it. Australian shepherds love their owners the same way they do everything else — by putting their whole heart into it.

From puppy to adult, an Aussie can be a fun part of life for many years.

Glossary

breed (BREED) — a certain kind of animal within an animal group; breed also means to mate and raise a certain kind of animal.

breeder (BREE-duhr) — someone who breeds and raises dogs or other animals

breed standard (BREED STAN-durd) — the physical features of a breed that judges look for in a dog show

conformation (kon-fawr-MEY-shun) — how well a dog meets its breed standard

hip dysplasia (HIP dis-PLAY-zhah) — a hip condition that affects the walking ability of some dogs

neuter (NOO-tur) — a veterinary operation that prevents a male dog from producing offspring

obedience (oh-BEE-dee-uhnss) — obeying rules and commands

protein (PROH-teen) — a substance found in all plants and animals; proteins help dogs stay healthy.

spay (SPEY) — a veterinary operation that prevents a female dog from producing offspring

vaccination (vak-suh-NAY-shun) — a shot of medicine that protects animals from a disease

Read More

Miller, Marie-Therese. *Hunting and Herding Dogs*. Dog Tales: True Stories about Amazing Dogs. New York: Chelsea Clubhouse, 2007.

Preszler, June. *Caring for Your Dog*. Positively Pets. Mankato, Minn.: Capstone Press, 2007.

Internet Sites

FactHound offers a safe, fun way to find Internet sites related to this book. All of the sites on FactHound have been researched by our staff.

Here's all you do:

Visit *www.facthound.com*

FactHound will fetch the best sites for you!

Index